With nearly a thousand years of history behind her, the ancient capital Thang Long and the present city of Hanoi, is proud to be one of the oldest and most elegant capital of South East Asia.

Being the heart of the country, Hanoi attracts the best of the cultural elite of Vietnam and of the Vietnamese.

Linked to the fate of the country, Hanoi has gone through a number of periods of change. However Hanoi has preserved itself as a focal point of "the sacred soul of the country" and represents the ideal of the vietnamese tradition : courage, générosity, elegance and authenticity ... Since the Ly, Tran, and Le dynasties... to the very first years of independance (1945), Hanoi has constantly stamped the historical pages of the country. Hanoi is an infinite subject, an endless inspiration for composers, poets and musicians.

Hanoi is a city being constantly reborn. With time, Hanoi will become bigger and more beautiful, until it reachs the level of the capitals of our friend countries , spread over the five continents. It will become the symbol of the vietnamese influence of this new era, to answer to the wishes of its inhabitants and of the whole vietnamese people.

Even engaged on the the path to modernisation, Hanoi will keep its unique caracter. People from Hanoi are welcoming, always ready to greet close or long-distant friends, to help them to admire a unique culture which represents the 53 ethnic groups which together make up the mother land. Friends who pass through Hanoi, you will find a deep peace, a charming and dreaming beauty; an "eternal" Hanoi.

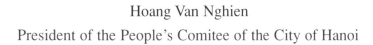

Hoang Van Nghien
President of the People's Comitee of the City of Hanoi

Thanks to the firms and organizations who made this book possible

Eternal Hanoï

CONTEMPORARY PORTRAIT OF A TIMELESS CITY

PHOTOGRAPHY BY THOMAS RENAUT
TEXT BY MICHEL HOÀNG

FOREWORD BY JEAN LACOUTURE

a pictorial book collection from

Les Editions d'Indochine

Hommage to the capitals of Indochina

Let us try, then, to imagine the cities and large villages of Indochina in the middle of the nineteenth century; Cochin China spreading along the banks of the Mekong.

Glimpses of sophisticated civilizations, where the grandeur of the Khmer empire merged with the native genius of the Vietnamese, and with the spirits of the great Mekong river, as it runs down from the highlands of Tibet...

We see a panoply of chrming cities, teeming with life, glowing with vegetation, where the flowers explode with color and vitality, flowers that would someday be called «les filles du consul.»

People were then only beginning to use the word «Indochine,» coined a few years earlier by the Danish geographer Conrad Malte-Brun.

The concept of Vietnam was hazier then, or at least its precise geographic expanse was fairly vague. Driving back the Khmer settlements, hardworking populations emerged from Hanoï and Hué to take up residence along the Mekong delta, offering a bountiful empire to Gia Long, first emperor of Vietnam (1802)- an empire built at the expense of the realm of the kings of Kampuchea, heirs to the founders of Angkor.

This was a world of shifting coalitions and budding potential, a world that the challenge of colonialism worked to reshape and awaken,and it was a world that i myself discovered in the wake of the war- I am referring to the Second World War- at the dawn of the great ensuing turmoil that in time brought forth Vietnam, Laos, and Cambodia, all of them independent, but all deeply seamed with scars and wounds.

Saigon, which was largely spared by the World War, still teemed with soldiers from the four corners of the earth, Japanese, British, French, and troops from the Gurkha Regiment.

Saigon still smiled through her suffering and fears, not so much lovely as she was coaxing and cajoling, and every bit as charming as she was captivating, juicy as a ripe mango, as rich and springy as raw latex. We were dazzled by the bright orange and scarlet flowers of the flame trees, while the colors of the colonial architecture- in which ochre and terracotta red were the prevailing hues- spoke to us with all kthe eloquence of a story by Roland Dorgelès, or a piece of reporting by a very young André Malraux.

No one unfamiliar with Saigon in those early years- the years before the French war, later an American war, transformed the town into a seedy R&R spot for troops recovering from bloody combat- could imagine the perfume of thrilling chance encounters and of leisure spiced with danger. Too many men were already dying in the vicinity, and foreign military intervention was already too objectionable, for one to be able to speak of «the good old days.»

And yet I am bound to bear witness to the poisonous allure of what I shall call «the days of datura, « if I may. It was there and then, in the last lingering days of my adolescence, that I tried to grasp and fathom another culture, another sensibility, another set of «rights.»

And one should not forget this, when visiting the huge modern-day city, swollen to its present size by two wars. Phnom Penh was the unremitting dream of those of us who worked in Saigon-a dream of a peaceful capital on the banks of the fabled Mekong. When, after a wait of four or five months, I was finally accorded entry into the town where a little king ruled under the name of Norodom Sihanouk Varman, I though I would die of joy: Phnom Penh was lovely, cheerful, broad and free, spacious and verdant. There was a lively spring in one's step in the years before the blighted curse of Pol Pot and his irregular assassins fell upon this gracious river town...

Of course, among the best and the brightest of Phnom Penh's youth, one could sense a lively impatience: the governing hand of France lay heavy, or at least it did until the «royal crusade» of 1953, and the rise to power of two young revolutionaries named Hou Youn and Chau Seng, who were later to die under the bludgeons of their former comrades of the Angkar. This and every other subject were addressed openly in the charming little outdoor cafés that dotted the shores of the lake of Tonlé-Sap or in the lovely little restaurants of the market, near the train station. Young Cambodia was jumping out of its skin, with a great unslakable thirst for life, and the country's capital, voluptuously stretching along riverbanks and lakeshores, seemed like some great exotic goddess of love, encouraging the youth to hope for a bright future. I spent much less time in Vientiane.This is surely due to the hard-headed good sense of the Laotians, who had no desire to upset the course of history. My most frequent stays in the Kingdom of a Million Elephants took place in the Plain of Jars, where the three princes, Souvanna Phouma, Souphannouvong, and Boun Oum, struggled - with relative success - to come to an accord. I try to remember the name of the little hotel in the Laotian capital where we would stop, impatiently rushing through our meal of rice and shrimp, so that we could

then emerge to saunter along the banks of the Mekong, watching the endless and yellow river waters... We planned our reporting so that we could spend as much time as possible admiring the exquisite Thai women, with their high breasts and splendid gestures of unadorned grace. And has Vientiane changed as much as Saigon and Phnom Penh? I do not know, but when a city is so much a reflection of its river, then it would be necessary to halt the waters in their flow before it could be sullied. And who would dare to imprison the Mekong?

To tell the truth, however, there is no city in Indochina that has so deeply moved me, charmed me, or captivated me as did Hanoï. Here, more than anywhere else, I witnessed the history of modern Indochina as it was being made, back in the remarkable year of 1946, when destiny hovered daily between peace and war. Peace lingered, so near and yet so unattainable, while bloody war threatened, a war that we could hardly imagine would last thirty years...

Returning to Hanoï just two years ago, I found, intact, my dear little Lake, the Temple of Literature, Silk Street, the countless cyclist who cut through the air like heroic dragonflies...

Hanoï, the brave and the faithful city ... Hanoï, which struggles step by step toward a veritable peace...

Jean Lacouture, Paris.

*W*hatever route you take to reach Hanoï, it will surprise you.

Whether you arrive in the capital of Vietnam by road or plane, each time you approach it you will get an initial impression of stark contrasts. The superannuated backdrop of a provincial tranquillity being elbowed aside by the feverish and laborious activity of the inhabitants.

The immediate surroundings of the city which stands in a wide plane, can be described as consisting of three interrelatedand interdependent complementary features complémentaires: water, land and rice. As the seasons change, vast areas of stagnant water divided by narrow earthworks stretching as far as the eye can see turn into muddy ponds from which the nostrils of buffalos occasionally emerge seeking fresh air among the patchwork of plots pierced by the tender green shoots of emerging rice plants. Here and there, at the appropriate times in the agricultural year, farmers bend over their crops, their feet embedded in the soggy soil, watching the reflections of passing clouds in the magical mirror of the

a perspective
of peasants
and family life

waters. Ploughing, harrowing, sowing, transplanting, replanting, weeding, flooding the fields, harvesting — all these rice cultivation tasks are still performed by manual labour just as the peasants have done for thousands of years, almost for eternity. It continues here right up to the outskirts of Hanoï, and how else can one approach and understand Vietnam without seeing it through its perspective of peasants and village and family life?

Quick lunch in the corn of the street.

The transition between the countryside surrounding Hanoï and the city itself is hardly sudden, as if the urban environment was a natural extension of the rice-paddies which surround it and which feed it. The ribbon of asphalt which brings to the city cyclists bearing armfuls of waterweed and motor-cycles with side-cars laden with poultry des seem to announce the immediate proximity of a country market town. The roadsides are bordered with little houses with badly fissured frontages and narrow, damp-eroded booths, brightly lit as soon as dusk begins to fall. They appear to be the harbingers of interminable outskirts which would seem to be heavily populated. One seems to be travelling through an interminable suburb, but one is already in the city itself. Arriving by the newly-built motorway, liking Noî Bâi airport with the capital, one's encounters with a few gleaming vehicles and the rather affected gestures of the officials in their bright new uniforms who operate the toll-booths lead to the conclusion that these are the portents of a predicted modernisation. But once you have covered the 2,000 or so yards (1800 metres) from Chuong Duong Bridge which cross the Red River parallel to the arachaic and imposing Long Biên steel suspension bridge, you soon realise your mistake. Behind the embankments which run alongside the river in its journey to the sea some 70 kilometres downstream, the fertile, brick-red soil, the extreme dilapidation of Trân Quang-Khai Avenue and the village-like atmosphere of the activity along its pavements de ses trottoirs all contribute to the impression that one is passing through a small town forgotten by 20th-century town-planning.

It is probably a futile exercise to compare Hanoï with the neighbouring metropolises of south-east Asia.. Compared with Bangkok, Hanoï has none of the proudly anarchic vitality, in which flashy and extravagant modernity has supplanted Siamese tradition completely. Compared with Kuala-Lumpur it has neither the uneasiness nor the opulence and bravery of that city's triumphal architecture triomphante. Compared with Singapore, capital of the Chinese diaspora, it displays none of the excessively westernised street layout and imposed urbanity. Nor has it the spaciousness and langour of Vientiane or the disparate personality and signs of recent wounds which tipify Phnom Penh. As for a comparison with Saigon, its eternal rival to the south, Hanoï cannot compete with its airy, sun-dappled town centre its lively commercial atmosphere, a tiny bit showy and rebellious.

A traditional image of Hanoï :
Small lake's loves

One enters Hanoï as if one were surreptiously strealing into a room whose shutters filter the raw glare of the light and attenuate the tumult outside the windows.

Hanoï does not scintillate, there is no affected allure, nor does it overwhelm with its grandiosity or magnificence, affectation or magnificence. With its islets of greenery, its lakes with their lotus-covered banks, avenues lined with tamarind and rôyâl trees which throw their peaceful shade over the facades of the old colonial buildings, Hanoï diffuses a subtle, discreet and even secret charm that is profoundly spellbinding. One does not admire Hanoï, one does not have a passing infatuation for the city. One becomes deeply attached to Hanoï.

REMENBRANCE OF THINGS PAST

Hanoï was founded in the eleventh century, making it the oldest capital city in south-east Asia. Although the vestiges of a prehistoric fort called Co-loa, dating from the third century b.c. has been excavated at the site, it was not until the seventh century a.d. that the kings of Vietnam built their cities along the Red River.

the oldest capital city in South-East Asia.

Tu-Thanh, La-Thanh, Dai-La, are all places built along the Great Lake, on the right bank of the river, in an ideal strategic position at the apex of the delta and the junction of roads and waterways. In 968 a.d., the Dinh and Le dynasties settled nearly 100 kilometres to the south, at Hoa-Lu, protected by a particularly convoluted limestone outcrop.

When the Ly conquered Hanoï, Vietnam became a Chinese vassal and remained so for a thousand years. In 1010, King Ly Thai-Tô felt himself to be powerful enough to found his new capital city to the north.

Early morning rice supply.

According to legend, as he leapt on to the riverbank at the landing-place, he spied a dragon taking flight. Hence the name of Thang Long (Dragon taking flight) as the old name for Hanoï. Dykes were built along the river bank to control the periodic flooding, and its tributaries were channelled to be used as irrigation ditches in the rice-paddies and to drain the marshes. But the founding of a royal city needed to obey the ritual imperatives dictated by Chinese geomancy and marks of favour from the guardian divinities. According to ancient beliefs a capital city, the seat of a sovereign ruling by Divine Right, must constitute an intermediary between the social order and the universal order.

The city was thus symbolically supported by its "magic mountain," the Three Summits (Ba Vi), 40 kilometres to the east, while it wore an aquatic belt in the form of tributaries of the river. The Tô Lich river was chosen as the home of water-sprite and as a shelter for the mountain spirit, mounds were built along astrological principles. All of the religious and official buildings were constructed on the principles of Fengshui, the geomantic principles which ensure that a building is erected in a lucky position.

Under the later dynasties of Ly, Trân and Lê there were several important monarchs. These include Le Loi, who was victorious against the Chinese and Lê Tuong-Duc who enriched the palace in the capital city.

In the seventeenth century, the Dutch and English set up trading posts in Hanoï but in the next century, wars and uprisings ravaged the city.

In 1802, the Nguyên princes established a capital at Hué and Thang Long, now reduced to a mere provincial capital, changed its name to Hanoï (on one side of the river). With its capture by the French in 1882, the colonial period began. There was considerable unrest in Hanoï during the period of resistance against French rule and between 1955 and 1975, it was the capital of a country split in two. In the années 1970s, it was subjected to repeated bombings by the Americans. It was not until 1975 that it regained its rightful place in a Vietnam that was finally reunited.

An Eternity Of Reprieve

When Hanoï's Hô Tây lake, formerly known as the Lake of Mists, finally emerges from its diaphanous fog, the dawn light which gardually chases away the shadows of the city to reveal the colours and shapes is a heavenly blessing on anyone who has had to rise early enough to witness the phenomenon. With this apparition, the city awakes. At the entrance to a street, the first cyclist takes to his wheels. Wearing a khaki-coloured helmet, a loose shirt over his trousers and sandals, he pedals silently towards a nearby office or distant workshop...Then suddenly, in the space of a minute and as if answering an invisible reveille, ten, twenty, fifty, a thousand cyclists

cover the roadway. The rarity of traffic lights ensures that road-users are constantly on the move. As a result, the traffic has to move intuitively, nose-to-tail. People overtake each other, brush against each other, criss-cross in every direction, in an anarchic ballet-on-wheels, yet often without doing the slightest damage, thanks to a disconcerting grace and coolheadedness.. The tide of cyclists is pursued by growling smoking Suzukis and Hondas, claiming their share of the asphalt. Behind the helmeted motorcycle-rider, passenger sit in xe om (arms around his waist) or he may have blocks of ice, charcoal or even a live pig strap-

how could this city ever be described as sad or austere

ped to the pillion. The great two-wheel invasion has begun. It will not stop until dusk. Now the pedlar-women arrive in their black-and-maroon suits, wearing scarves or straw hats, winter and summer, with their packs on yokes. The heavy load gives them a distinctive walk, a sort of leaping gait, punctuated with a jerk of the arm. They reach their regular pitch and squat behind it.

One of the best street markets in Asia is Dông Xûan Market, a feast for the eye, nose and palate, full of exquisite smells and tastes. The absence of freezers and modern packaging expose long-forgotten aromas and odours, the effluvia, steam, emissions and even stenches.

Unidentified rolling objets can be easily found in the city.

In the meat market, dismembered pigs have become carmine pork joints, glazed quarters, a heap of purplish offal, cubes of trembling lard or bunches of sweetish sausages. Further on, there is the powerful odour of live crabs and fish. The fruit market reeks of the acid aroma of green oranges from Vinh, against the sweetish odour of miniature bananas from Nam-Dinh, and the syrupy fragrance of translucent lychees. Here also are succulent mangosteens, the nauseating reek of the durian and the soft and creamy flesh of the jackfruit.

In the hustle and bustle of trade, one is diverted to the stalls displaying china, firecrackers or votive objects. The religious articles are piled in heaps of joss-sticks, artificial gold ingots and fake banknotes, items which are burned during funeral rites.

It is in these markets, these crowded alleyways bustling with little workshops, that the heart of the city beats. The tiny shops and stalls are run by peasants who have turned themselves into bicycle repairers or tyre-pumpers. This is where one discovers the cheeky humour, irony and good or bad temper of the residents of Hanoi. How could this city ever be described as sad or austere? Is it because of its despoliation, the dilapidation of the house frontages? How could its inhabitants be described as distant and remote? Is it due to their false pride which stops them from inviting a stranger into the decrepit, crumbling villas in

14

which they live, buildings which have been split up in order to accommodate four families? Or perhaps because, between December and February, a constant drizzle envelops the city in a misty, ill-defined dampness? Winter is also the season of the lunar New Year, celebrated with a modest display of multicoloured illuminations surmounting the elegant curve of the vermillion wooden bridge over the reclaimed Sword Lake. These are pleasantly watered evenings, which last until the last revellers leave with a final burst of firecrackers.

At lunchtime, that is to say, all day, people crowd into the little restaurants which have opened almost everywhere since 1986, when the authorities began to allow private trade. A charcoal brazier, a couple of big pots and a few sticks of wood have become a com-pho (rice and soup). Seated on a miniature stool, a spicy pho, Hanoï's famous soup, warms the stomach and the heart. A hundred yards away, a mirror hanging from a nail and an armchair create a barber's and the blare of karaoke music from a tiny doorway becomes a bistro where you can order a ca-phe kem (café-crème) or a ba-ba-ba (333) beer. It is not until the cool of the evening that the bustle calms down and domestic life resumes in the residential quarters. At the foot of a nettle-tree (an oriental species of elm), bearded old men wearing French berets play cards, grandmothers with toddlers on their knees take the air and schoolchildren bend over their homework by the light of a bare bulb. Urban life implodes, revolving around its original nucleus, the family.

Hanoïs is decidedly a modest city which does not expose itself and does not seek to scandalise or amaze. In any case, how could it afford to do so? It is not very cosmopolitan and has a rather provincial atmosphere, but it needs to modernise and transform itself. The dilapidation of the buildings, the broken drains, the old-fashioned utilities and indigenous technology all mean that there will have to be important changes in the future. How will they be handled? The few examples of westernisation, such as the buildings erected with aid from the former Eastern bloc, have not always been happy ones and even if admiration and vene-

The shape of Vietnam has often been compared to a dragon.

ration for President Hô Chi-Minh still remain intact here, his massive Moscow-style mausoleum was not received with unanimous acclaim. Modernisation (normal) is posing quite a few questions as to the future of the city. Should it be opened up to the market economy, to ASEAN, to tourism and consequently to foreign capital, thus inviting or inciting major transformations? There is a recognition here that a valuable city heritage needs to be preserved without alteration and that any modernisation must harmonise, there must be no banality of concrete or pettiness of grandiose megaliths. The quality of life and the soul of city must be preserved. Hanoï is not incorruptible. Let us hope that it remains unsinkable and does not become submerged in unrestrained and unlovable modernism, as impersonal as it is inhuman. Let it never be said of Hanoï in the future - as the poet Pham Quy-Tich once said of the lovely Kiêu - "its beauty did not deserve to be drowned".

architecture

When the French took over Hanoi, the city lost much of its sparkle, being usurped as the capital by Hué. But the French wanted to turn it into a resolutely modern city, as they had done with Saigon. In 1886, when the governor, Paul Bert, inaugurated the major rebuilding, he declared: "The hordes of natives had to be subjugated and shown the indisputable superiority of the new power, while ensuring its enduring nature. The Sthird Republic must remain imperial in the style of Baron Haussmann. Without a second thought, the citadel is razed to the ground, as are the pagodas and the old districts in order to replace them with government buildings, barracks and the homes of the colonists". After 1905, the governor-general, Paul Doumer, deplored this destruction. "That we were wrong to demolish the gates of the citadel, there is no doubt.

Hanoï is rich of a well preserved heritage.

Were we right to demolish the citadel itself, to smash the centuries-old, massive ramparts, built to last indefinitely?... The disappearance of those gates will only be an irritation for art and history."

The buildings in the colonial districts of the Concession and the Citadel have remained almost intact. This gives them a very French look, but one which evokes that old-fashioned French urban architecture, the sort of outmoded, provincial style reminiscent of such towns as Pau, Deauville or Biarritz, looking like something from an early sepia photograph of yesteryear.

If the pompous government buildings and follies in "pagodaed Normand" architecture look like clumsily constructed wedding-cakes, there are nevertheless many attractive edifices. After the academic style of the nineteenth century, came architects such as Hébrard, Vildieu and Nguyên Cao-Luyên whose work was often original and modernist. Art Nouveau and geometrical shapes after the Mallet-Stevens Art Deco school stand side-by-side with that indefinable "colonial" style vaguely inspired by the indigenous architecture.

Ochre, saffron or celadon green villas conceal secret gardens, some carefully nurtured, others unkempt, like little transplanted corners of France, in which the only exotic touch is the background of mango trees or, in May, the bright red of the flamboyants. From the Great Lake to the Little Lake, through Hoàng Diêu Street, Tràng Thi Street and their surroundings, the scene looks like something out of a novel set in French Indochina. But the war and the impoverishment of the tenants of the Hanoï municipality have allowed damp to invade the buildings. Stone and plaster, brick and concrete are covered with the strange map-like expanses of lichen and moss. In the commercial district of the "Thirty-six Corporations" the bungalows reveal, under their lopsided roofs, cracked pediments, balconies et balustrades and cornices, buttresses and keystones whose plaster is badly cracked.

The intimidating architecture of the Hô Chi Minh mausoleum.

But Hanoï is also the memory of earlier times. There is the unique pagoda on stilts, a marvel of grace emerging from lotus buds. It is the temple of literature in which giant stone tortoises carry on their backs stone tablets engraved with Chinese characters extolling the glories of the mandarins of old. It is the patina on the ancient woodwork of the temples of Voi Phuc or Quan Thành. And it is the charm of the little pagoda, emerging from the middle of the Little Lake, which surrounded by swirling morning mists, looks like something out of a oriental woodcut.

Yet how can one ignore the general dilapidation of the surroundings or the promiscuity, ugliness and sadness of some of the buildings on the outskirts? Could they be modernised, rehabilitated or rebuilt without disturbing too greatly the vestiges of colonisation or ruining the rich architectural and historic heritage ?

*Now topped by the red flag with the gold star, the for-
mer residence, with its ornate mouldings and handso-
me awning overhanging the cornice, is an example
of official French architecture.*

The grand staircase of the former palace of the "Gougal" is illuminated from the skylight above it.

At the Fine Arts Museum, which contains magnificent collections of the crafts of ethnic minorities, the outdoor galleries offer a delightful alternation between areas of light and shade.

Despite the weathering they have suffered, the yellow and white of these "colonial" villas are part of a harmonious architectural patchwork.

Green moss which flourishes in the cool, damp winters, creeps up a staircase above the cream-coloured facades of houses in which Asiatic roofs are combined with European-style balconies.

Fish are used to decorate the veranda of an Art Deco residence whose off-centre shapes are reminiscent of the Mallet-Stevens style.

This quaint little folly, with its rotunda, pierced stone work, bulls-eye window, and arches stands "where, along the wide avenues, pompous, hybrid and pretentious villas look as if they had been transported straight from the Cote d'Azur or Italy" (Claude Palazzoli, Le Viet-Nam entre deux mythes).

This long gallery is open to the sun, between indoors and outdoors, and is intricately carved with Chinese good luck symbols.

These open shutters reveal a garden and under a roof covered with Bordeaux tiles, a house whose porch is decorated with the Chinese character "fu" (prosperity).

The Grand Theatre at the entrance to Trang Tien Street
was opened in 1901. Its ochre-coloured stonework
marries well with the bank of greenery beside it.

An imposing double coil of steps leads to the waiting room of the courthouse built in 1906.

The peaceful intimacy of a miniature garden growing in china pots demonstrates the love of the people of Hanoi for nature and the tropical vegetation which pervades their city.

The glazed tiles of an arched roof overhanging a balcony with a balustrade is an example of a composite style which has become known as "colonial".

The tip of a pointed roof can be seen from a window, pointing at a facade decorated with a Chinese good luck symbol.

This unusual double window, with its accoladed lintel and wooden shutters with their projecting wooden lathes is decorated with unexpected patterns.

The Grand Hall of the History Museum (formerly the Louis Finot Museum), whose gallery is supported on a triple colonnade, is a foretaste of the magnificent collections acquired by the prestigious Ecole Française d'Extrême-Orient.

A moulded plaster ceiling, marble-clad walls, double
pillars and Corinthian columns of porphyry, double
chandeliers with fans above a bust of Hô Chi-Minh...
an extraordinary and unfathomable collection of
styles.

This aerial view of Hanoi reveals its archaic, faded air which various international bodies plan to rehabilitate, while hoping to retain the atmosphere of the locality.

The Museum of History's hexagonal rotunda, its roof decorated with fancy tiles shaped like dragons and its beautiful galleries, constitute a surprisingly successful mixture of styles.

Top : *Behind the decrepitude of its frontage of columns in a mixture of styles, this old house is probably home to three or four families who survive without any modern conveniences.*

Bottom : *Some owners have preserved and restaured a vivid architecture. Here the Hôtel Sofitel Metropole in the center of the city.*

Right : *A refreshing bath into west-lake waters at the end of the day, in Hanoï, temperature can easily reach 40°C.*

The Directorate of Finance is a perfect example of a colonial-style building. It combines its facade of European-style balustrades with a roof in Far Eastern style and is shaded with beautiful foliage.

The shrubbery of a shady patio reveals the ambulatory of an ancient monastery which contained a religious hospital.

Top : *If crosswinds filter the sun's rays, leaving the interior of this home in the cool shade, its yellow roughcast plasterwork looks like a valley of light.*

Bottom : *This Buddhist stupa at the entrance to a house consists of lotus buds framing a metal lily-of-the-valley resting on a heart. Are these symbols intended for the visitor?*

Top : *This blue balustrade in quarter-rounds, bricks with a convex surface and potted plants amidst luxuriant greenery create an almost theatrical decor at the end of a cul-de-sac.*

Bottom: *Whose ghosts live behind this balcony, this brightly coloured balustrade and these French-style shutters, covered in mouldering damp?*

t r a d i t i o n s

Vietnam is at the crossroads of two great cultures, Indian and Chinese. It is here that inhabitants of very diverse cultures have been thrown together and forced to mix. It is thus a land of syncretism. Be this as it may, most of the beliefs, institutions, architecture, arts, literature and even the calendar have been inspired by China.

Back from work on the former Doumer Bidge.

The religious traditions are closely tied to the calendar which marks the important rituals with the passing seasons. The mid-autumn festivals is one of the of great importance. There are parades with music, toys and coloured paper figurines are purchased for the children who are stuffed with cakes and pastries. This is also the wedding season. The Thanh-Minh (Pure Clarity) Festival is also of Chinese origin. It is the Chinese Day of the Dead, when families visit the mausoleums together There are also official holidays of more recent origin, such as Independence Day, when statesmen and political leaders gather in Ba-Dinh Square and foreign delegations and soldiers are present, surrounded by scarlet emblems.

But the Têt estival, Chinese New Year, is the highlight of the year. It falls in late January or early February, and while it is being celebrated all public actvity grinds to a halt. The citizens of Hanoï prepare for the occasion with feverish buying sprees, and for at least three days, they spend all their time visiting their nearest and dearest and travelling to see relatives living in the provinces. Planes, trains and public entertainments are booked solid. Depending on their means, the Vietnamese gorge on, or at least partake of, a few special dishes and share the banh-chung (New Year cake, a sweet rice-cake), not without having honoured and symbolically fed the ancestors. Then there are card games, the favourite pasttime of the crowded streets, visits to street-photographers, and a trip to the theatre to see a traditional entertainment. Mischievous, joyful young women carry branches of burgeoning buds symbolising the spring. They prance *gaily along the shores of Lake Hoan Kiêm or through Lenin Park in their ao-dai. Fireworks, the machine-gun exhaust of the motorbikes and firecrackers set off by children burst through the silence of the night.*

Hanoï gives itself up to pleasure. This is a happy, joyful occasion, enjoyed by all classes, a social and sociable festivity which outshines all the western festive occasions with their tawdry commercialism. In Hanoï the Têt retains its tradition as a genuine celebration.

The historian, Nguyên Khac-VViên described Hanoi, with its countryfied aspects and recently urbanised population as "a village turning into a town". The family is still the focal point of society and remains the preserver and observer of tradition. The family clan still retains its Confucian, patriarchal importance, deciding the future of the younger generation and arranging marriages. Although the woman is an empress in the home, she still plays her traditional role. Yet her situation has changed due to such factors as war, education, work and a measure of economic independence, all of which have contributed to reinforcing the socialist doctrine of the emancipation of women. But urbanisation, the growing influence of the media and westernisation have added their own impetus for change. The women of Hanoï are having to consider their future position very carefully.

By definition, traditions are required to be self-perpetuating. Yet they also evolve, and who knows for how long the lines penned by the sixteenth-century poet, Nguyên Gian-Thanh, will remain true:

"Many countries build their power on their fortresses.

Let us rather make the virtues of justice and humanity our ramparts.

To see, generation after generation, Spring after spring,

Our children transmit our beautiful traditions for a thousand, ten thousand years" ?

Morning training to the art of fight (Wu-Shu).

"Who could know, as he did, how many lakes there
were in Hanoï, both big and small".
(Bao Ninh : The Sorrow of War)

Winding alleyways, washing hanging out, bicycles,
street urchins.... an almost Neapolitan atmosphere in
which only the bicycle thieves are missing.

Left : *Peering through the cloud of make he has created, a bevoter enjoys the pleasures of the hookah.*

Top: *Old memories and fresh news... the delights of tropical languor as if one were lounging on the shores of the Mediterranean.*

Bottom: *Cigarettes are sold by the piece, tiny cups of jasmine tea, a small can of beer.. like the pedlars of yesteryear. The only touch of modernity is the electronic calculator.*

This bicycle has a long way to travel until it reaches the radiant future of mechanised industry.

Quails' eggs, a hand of bananas, sweets, violet and indigo velvet, jade, gold or scarlet satin... this Hanoï beauty wearing the traditional "khan vuong" headdress presides over a marketplace in microcosm.

Top : *Billiards are a very popular pastime - played here in the Anglo-American style - and the table can be set up at any street corner. There is heavy betting on the outcome of the matches.*

Bottom: *These little girls jumping over an elastic skipping-rope are among the forty per cent of Vietnamese now aged under twenty.*

The dictum "dong nhu dam choi ga" (as big a crowd as at a cock fight) still remains true. The villages of Van-dinh and Thuy-chuong have long been famous for the aggressiveness of their roosters.

Left : *As soon as the weather turns cold
the sensitivity of the townspeople manifests itself.
Once the temperature drops to 15°C (60°F), the fake fur
hats come out of the closet.*

Right : *Hats come in all shapes and sizes, made of palm,
pineapple or bamboo leaves, pot - or basket - shaped or
looking like an elephants' foot. The baseball cap has not
supplanted them all yet, as has happened in Saigon.*

Left : The light "boi doi" forage cap, headgear which has not gone out of style for half a century. Soldiers simply pin a little red star to it.

Right : A young student wearing the traditional satin dress smiles into the future. She had only just been born when the war ended and has the right to hope for a happier life than her parents have had.

The Vietnamese language has half a dozen words to designate the popular pastime of kite-flying. They include double fairy, banyan leaf, swallow or tank top.

Couples take boats out on the Ho Tai (Western Lake) right up until dusk, seeing romantic isolation.

*Domestic appliances are still so outdated that
cooking-stoves are still fuelled with anthracite dust
from the Hong-gay mines, which are compacted into
cylinders by workmen.*

There is excellent fishing in the multitude of lakes to be found throughout Hanoi. The wonderful aroma of nuoc-nam , a fermented fish sauce, pervades many alleyways.

Sunday in Hanoï: a hairdresser has chosen not to make this a rest day, while on the corner of an avenue, the tyre repairer and a seller of petrol (gasoline) by the litre hope for an unfortunate motorcyclist.

Craftsmen crouch on the pavement to repair a piece of furniture inlaid with mother-of-pearl. This highly skilled job has given its name to a famous street, Inlayers' Street.

Behind the street scenes, hidden away from all but prying eyes, Vietnamese women continue their unremitting, back-breaking toil, caused by the lack of even the most basic appliances.

When the Tet, the Lunar New Year, is celebrated, kumquat plants, and especially cay-mai (plum-tree) buds are traditional presents which bring good luck.

"In the peasant market, there was a wide variety of delicious snacks... Next to grilled, honey-coated sweetcorn kernels, there were stews of young rice shoots, stews flavoured with five-spice and fritters shaped like caterpillars ". (Duong Thu-Huong, The blind paradises).

Following page : An ancien bronze tripod in the seventeenth- century Ambassador's Pagoda. The Pagoda is now used for Buddhist woror-ship and for buddhist advanced *religious studies*

religion

Officially, the Vietnamese are Buddhists. Yet there are household gods, altars dedicated to the ancestors, Confucian and Taoist temples, Roman Catholic churches and despite the state's official atheism, all these

continue to flourish. No doubt it is because Vietnam is a land of multiple religions. From time immemorial, it has retained a complex, animistic religion onto which it has grafted foreign beliefs. It imported Buddhism from India, Confucianism and Taoism from China and Christianity from the West.

This explains the simultaneous existence of household rites and public worship. Animism still flourishes and seeks, through various rituals, harmony between the celestial, terrestrial and human worlds. Hence, inside so many homes, offerings of alcohol, fruit and flowers are made to the god of the soil,Thô Công whose

New year colorful flags

altar is level with the ground and is lit by candles and even by electric fairy-lights.

Ancestor worship is associated with a cardinal virtue, that of filial piety. It results from a belief in the survival of part of the souls of the dead. These altars are raised above the ground, and are decorated with flowers. Joss-sticks embedded in bowls of rice are burned before the names or photographs of the deceased who are enjoined to protect their descendants. This is a basic socio-familial rite, one which is not linked to any particular religion.

There are a few Buddhist temples here and there, such as that of Ba-da, at which statues of Buddhas of the past (A Di Da), of the present (Thich Ca Mau Nhi) and the future (Di Lac) are venerated. Worshippers often pray to the Boddhisattvas, saints admitted to Nirvana and thus released from the cycle of reincarnations with their accompanying sorrows, but who have chosen to remain among human beings in order to help them achieve spiritual perfection. In the overpowering perfume of the spiralling smoke from the incen-

se, most of the worshippers can be seen to be women. Although there are fewer monks than in Cambodia or Thailand, their communities still have a part to play.

These same temples house Taoist divinities such as Ngoc Hoang, the Jade Emperor and his Immortals. The great principles of Taoism are metaphysical mediation and a balance between Man and Nature, between the feminine yin and the masculine yang.

Confucianism is more a code of ethics than a religion. It favours family and social cohesion and even political consensus through a strict respect for social distinctions and moral duties. Thus virtuous mandarins and brave patriots have been accorded divine status and are associated with temples.

All these beliefs and rites are interpreted and performed without the slightest apparent feeling of contradiction because dogmatism is quite out of place here.

Behind these open doors, a small private Pagoda.

The same cannot be said of Christianity, introduced by French and Spanish missionaries, since by its very nature, Christianity prohibits any other religious belief and practice. Despite its initial rejection by the authorities when the Europeans first arrived, and during the Ngo Dinh-Diem dictatorship from 1955 to 1963, based on fiercely anti-communist Roman Catholicism, Christianity has made millions of converts. The main seat of worship and the Hanoï diocese is St. Joseph's Cathedral, a neo-gothic curiosity with touches in the style of Viollet-le-Duc. There are plenty of worshippers although it is true that Vietnamese catholics do not always adhere strictly to monotheism. In many Christian homes, next to a biblical figure, stands the statuette of Quan Am, the Buddhist god of compassion, there may be an altar dedicated to Tho Cong, decorated with tangerines and little bowls or rice wine.

*At the entrance to the temple, kneeling elephants in
stone are a reminder of prince Linh Lang's victory
over the Chinese in the deventh century. The prince
led an impetuous charge of armed pachyderms.*

The roofs of the temples and pagodas shaped like buffalo horns reach up to the sky.

Behind a bronze incense-burner and a panoply of
halbards stards, a Chinese altar painted red, gold
and blue.

The simplicity of a household altar on which offerings of flowers, joss-sticks and a plastic carp - the symbol of longevity - bought from a toyseller have been laid.

Above: *The tolerance which the authorities have recently displayed has made it possible for a large number of communities of Buddhist nuns to establish themselves in several regions of the country.*

Right: *This young boy wears a mourning band and is about to take part in one of the three important ceremonies which follow a death, the rites of the third, 49th and 100th days.*

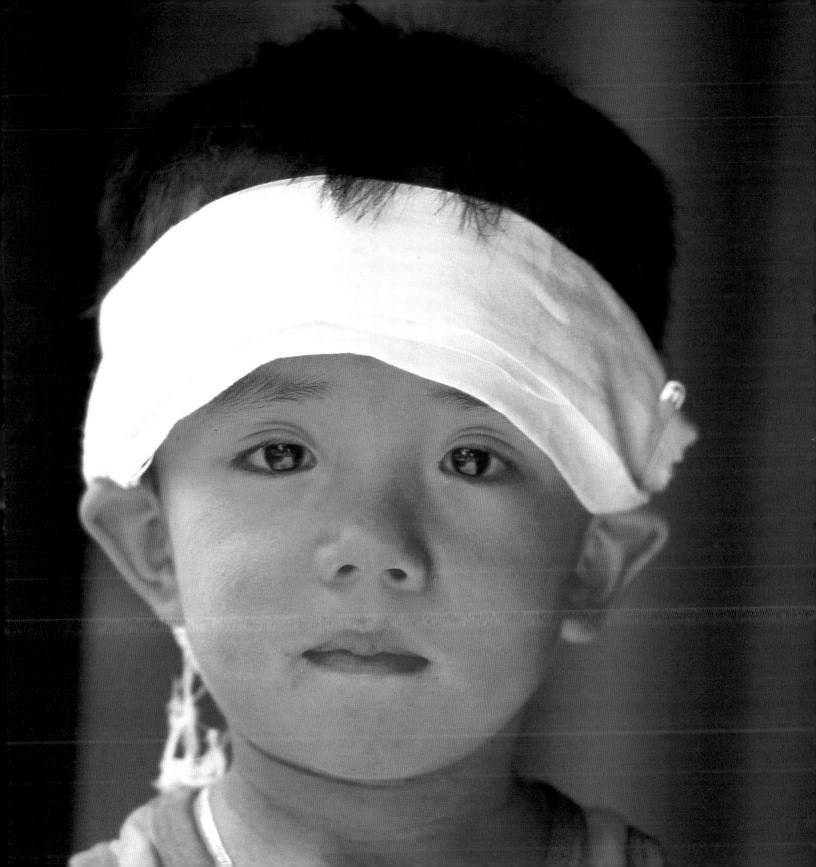

A carved wooden dragon faces the Chinese character
de - duc *in Vietnamese ("virtue") against a back-*
ground of right-facing swastikas, the Buddhist
symbols of good luck.

Craftsmen take infinite pains to repair the statue of a Buddhist divinity, while other silver-covered statuettes wait to be placed on an altar.

Young girls sing hymns to St. Joseph.
The Roman Catholic community consists of several
million worshippers.

Top: *A small Roman Catholic church in the suburbs bears a surprising resemblance to the Christian missions in Hispanic countries such as Mexico or the Philippines.*

Bottom: *This priest standing before his parishioners has little difficulty about celebrating the mass, since the authorities now guarantee both freedom of worship and atheism.*

Left: *St. Joseph's Cathedral was dedicated at*
Christmas, 1886 by Monsignor Puginier. It stands on
the vestiges of a pagoda which was rased to the
ground by the French occupying power.

Above: *Worshippers leaving Sunday mass. Most are*
women, who are in the habit of gathering in a circle
around a statue of the Virgin to sing hymns together.

Top: *Inside a Buddhist temple, the fabric covering a door is the same saffron colour as the robes of the monks who are gradually re-establishing congregations of worshippers.*

Bottom: *This pointed door is guarded by menacing warriors who use their halbards to prevent evil spirits from entering the temple.*

*A woman is praying at the altar of the Ambassadors'
Temple to the statue of Quan Am, the Buddhist god of
compassion, who extends his "thousand" arms to
alleviate human suffering.*

Left: *This guardian of the temple is allowed to retain his beard, an attribute traditionally reserved for old men because it signifies experience and thus moral wisdom.*

Right: *Joss-sticks are among the votive objects which are burned on altars or, as here, in front of a funerary alcove.*

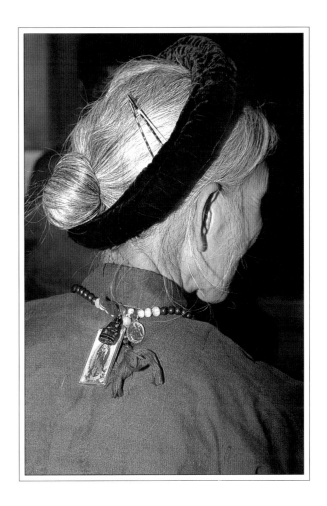

Left: *At the Taoist Temple of the White Horse (Den Bach ma), a votive pennant hangs next to the altar to a deified genii who is depicted as a white horse, the symbol of the sun star.*

Right: *This old lady wears the "khan giai", a traditional velvet band worn during ceremonies, and she has wound a chaplet covered with Buddhist images around her neck.*

Market gardeners squat before their fruit-stalls. The sign above the door is the stylised Chinese ideogram symbolising longevity.

92

Mourning is a demanding ritual in Vietnam, here some old ladies are preparing flower crowns.

Published in Paris in 1997 by
Les Editions d'Indochine - Asa Editions
Photographs : Thomas Renaut
Text : Michel Hoàng
Foreword : Jean Lacouture

Information regarding this publication and its dis-
tribution can be obtained by fax in Paris
Asa Editions
5 rue rennequin 75017 Paris France
Tèl : 01 92 27 75 00
Fax : 01 92 27 75 05

Publisher : Marc Wiltz
Conception : Thomas Renaut

ISBN: 2-911589-01-7
Publisher number: 2-911589
Distribution Vietnam : Fahasa
Traduction : Chanterelle Ltd.

Thanks to Bui Nghia, Tran Dinh Binh, Alexus
Hoàng, Mr Degallaix, ambassadeur de France,
George Hirsch, Jean-Pierre Vandenhende, Jean
Loup Cherel, François Amman et Christèle
Thomas, Guy de la Chevalerie, Cyril Lapointe,
Nicolas Arcilla Borraz, Laurent de Segonzac, Jean
Pierre Ducrest, Françoise Chappuis, Bernard
Broisin Doutaz, Myriam Laidet, Rémi Boutinet,
Farahnaz Leblais, Geneviève Piot Coliche, Jean
Charroing, Dominique Natot.

ALCATEL

Alcatel in involved in Vietnam since more than ten years.
In partnership with the Vietnamese Post and Telecommunications ,
Alcatel Network System Vietnam built each year over 200 000 lines
and is active on all communication sectors: transmission
systems, cables, GSM, PABX, access systems.

Employing over hundred people, Alcatel offers to its mana-
gers and workers technical training programs and language
facilities in France. ASNV has become the
showroom of the successfull partnership where the key
of this success has to be found in a long-term perspective.

That's why Alcatel is proud to be associated to the
publication of *Eternal Hanoï*. To show its involvement
in the cultural and human heritage of the capital, but
also to enhance its long-term action in Vietnam and its
confidence in the future of the country.

ASSIMIL, a pioneer in the self-study of modern languages, has over 65 years of experience in this field and is present in 70 countries.

With our basic principle of intuitive assimilation based upon short, varied and lively dialogues, our world famous methods allow you to reach the level of basic conversation, and help you acquire an intuitive feel for a new language.
In just a few months, with only 30 minutes of relaxed study per day, you will be able to get by in everyday situations. And you will have no problem of comprehension, because the high quality recordings that accompany the book capture the natural rhythms and music of the language.

Assimil has a long tradition of spreading knowledge of most world languages and cultures. Also, because of our recent involvement in developing specific methods for learning Vietnamese, we are proud to take part in this book, which enhances the cultural, human and religious heritage of the town of Hanoï.

The Ile-de-France region is strong of one third of the gross french income, represents more than 500.000 companies and half of the french research capacity, is a showroom of the french technology as well as the french culture. The region concentrates many factors of success and whishes to share it with Hanoï, "eternal city".

A cooperation agreement has been signed with the town of Hanoi in 1989.

Exchanges have been developped in different sectors : economy, urban planning, transportation, communication and computer science, professionnal training programs, culture and education.

This book enhances the uniqueness and the beauty of Hanoi ; it adds a new testimony to the Region attachment to this major capital city and its inhabitants.

Michel Giraud
Président du Conseil Régional
d'Ile-de-France

Vietnam's first five-star property, the Hotel Sofitel Metropole Hanoi is an award-winning French colonial-style hotel lying in the heart of Hanoi, near Hoan Kiem Lake and the magnificent Opera House.

Built at the turn of the century, the hotel boasts all the hallmarks of its era - a classic white facade, bottle-green shutters and wrought iron detail, interior wood panelling and a lush courtyard lawn. It also offers a traditional Vietnamese hospitality which has charmed the ambassadors, writers, war correspondents and entrepreneurs who have filled its rooms and bars since the beginning of the century.

Under Accor Asia Pacific management the hotel's facilities have been modernised, but the property still retains its old world charm and continues to attract heads of state, world leaders, royalty and celebrities from around the world.

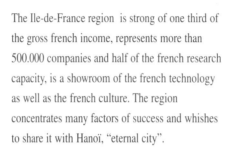